DON'T TELL ANYONE

Other Hollyridge Press Chapbooks by Tony Hoagland

Hard Rain
Little Oceans

Don't Tell Anyone

Anyone

A Chapbook

Tony Hoagland

Hollyridge Press
Venice, California

Hollyridge Press
Venice, California
www.hollyridgepress.com

Cover and Book Design by Rio Smyth
Cover Image © Pklimenko | Dreamstime.com
Author photo by Anne Stavley
Manufactured in the United States of America by Lightning Source

ISBN-13: 978-0-9843100-7-4
ISBN-10: 0-9843100-7-X

Acknowledgments

Thanks to the editors and the magazines in which these poems first appeared:

Poetry Magazine: "Summer," "Don't Tell Anyone," "There Is No Word"
American Poetry Review: "Aubade," "High Heels," "Wetness," "Application
    For Release from the Dream"
The Cortland Review: "His Majesty"
The Sun Magazine: "The Social Life of Water," "Summer Dusk," "A
    History of High Heels"
The Threepenny Review: "Wine Dark Sea"
Ploughshares: "December, With Antlers," "The Complex Sentence"
Fifth Wednesday Journal: "Wrong Question"
Green Mountains Review: "Proportion"
The Baffler: "Summit Meeting"
The Paris Review: "Write Whiter"
New Ohio Review: "Ode to the Republic"

21 20 19 18 17 16 15 14   10 9 8 7 6 5 4 3 2 1

Contents

Don't Tell Anyone

SUMMER

The tourists are strolling down Alpine Street
hoping for a deal on hand-carved rocking chairs

or some bronze Kali Yuga earrings
from the local Yak Arts dealer.

It's summer. No one needs therapy for now,
or a new translation of Proust

—laughing as they walk past the acupuncture clinic,
and *Orleans Fish and Chips*,

then double back to the Omega store
to look more closely at those shoes.

People like to buy. They just do.
They like the green tissue paper.

They like extracting the card from its tight
prophylactic sheath, handing it over,

and getting it back.
They like to swing the bag when they stroll away.

They like to stash the box in the car.
A forty-year old man stares at a wetsuit on the rack:

Is it too late in life to dress up like a seal and surf?
as the beech tree in front of the courthouse suddenly
                                        fluffs itself up and flutters,

and a woman with a henna rinse
holds a small glass vase up to the light

to see the tiny turquoise bubbles trapped inside.
As a child she felt a secret just inside her skin,

always on the brink of bursting out.
Now the secret is on the outside,

and she is hunting it.

HIS MAJESTY

What does His Majesty Mr.-Boombox-In-My-Jeep think
as he drives the beach road every night, at two A.M.,

under the bleached shell of the summer moon,
assaulting all the houses with his rude tunes?

Is that boom-boom-boom a cry for help? Is it
the kill song of a hunting shark, or

is that a neuro-limbic-node-blastoma I detect
spreading like junk food through the cheap

software of the American soul?

Attila the Hun, in your combat-camouflaged new Jeep,
white boy pretending to be black, or underprivileged, or street,

driving slow enough to wreck the sleep of these
retired, pajama-wearing citizens,

                                        what is wrong with you?

I bet I'm not the only one to hope his vehicle might flip
at the zigzag bend of the canal

and toss him headfirst in the swamp,
                                        where the dreadlocked mangrove roots
will seek and suck the Rastafarian right out of him.

Oh peaceful, divine Florida night,
mesmeric waves shimmering with lunar light,

Won't you rise up now and take your beauty back?
Won't you inflict the human condition with a big flat tire

or write it a ticket for two thousand years
                                    of disturbing the peace?
Won't you make the little people all sit down for a minute

and listen to the music
of the spacious, frightening concert of this living night?

DON'T TELL ANYONE

We had been married for six or seven years
when my wife, standing in the kitchen one afternoon, told me
that she screams underwater when she swims—

that, in fact, she has been screaming for years
into the blue chlorinated water of the community pool
where she does laps every other day.

Buttering her toast, not as if she had been
concealing anything,
not as if I should consider myself

personally the cause of her screaming,
nor as if we should perform an act of therapy
right that minute on the kitchen table,

—casually, she told me,
and I could see her turn her square face up
to take a gulp of oxygen,

then down again into the cold wet mask of the unconscious.
For all I know, maybe everyone is screaming silently
as they go through life,

politely keeping the big secret
that it is not all fun
to be ripped by the crooked beak

of what they call *psychology*,
to be dipped down
again and again into time;

that the truest, most intimate
pleasure you can sometimes find
is the wet kiss

of your own pain.
There goes Kath, at one P.M., to swim her 22 laps
back and forth in the community pool;

—what discipline she has!
Twenty-two laps like twenty-two pages,
that will never be read by anyone.

BECAUSE IT IS HOUSTON,

the streetlights have to take the place
usually reserved for the moon in the poem

and the traffic in the background with its roar and surge
stands in for the ocean
                        tossing wrecks like driftwood on the shore.

Because it is Houston, the
polished little blond talking on her cell phone

while backing her SUV at high speed through the parking lot
is a respected citizen

and the gnarled, serpentine, yearned-out limbs of oaks
above certain shady boulevards

suggest that even ugly can be beautiful.

Because it is Houston,
a moist wind blowing from the south at dawn

carries the faint petrochemical bouquet
                        from the landfills of our fathers
                                and the landfills of their fathers.
So sweet it smells!

A morning shower
has knocked down blossoms from the honeysuckle bush
                                into the grass
like little ivory trumpets.

Because there is no one better qualified around,
                                    because it is Houston,

you are the one who gets to kneel
upon the buckled sidewalk

and look at them in silence.

THE SOCIAL LIFE OF WATER

All water is a part of other water.
Cloud talks to lake; mist
speaks quietly to creek.

Lake says something back to cloud,
and cloud listens.
No water is lonely water.

All water is a part of other water.
River rushes to reunite with ocean;
Tree drinks rain and sweats out dew;
Dew takes elevator into cloud;
Cloud marries puddle. Puddle

has long conversation with lake about fiord;
Fog sneaks up and murmurs insinuations to swamp;
Swamp makes needs known to marshland;

Thunderstorm throws itself on estuary;
Waterspout laughs at joke of frog pond.
All water understands.

All water understands.
Reservoir gathers information
for database of watershed;
Brook translates lake to waterfall;
Tide wrinkles its green forehead and then breaks through.
All water understands.

But you, you stand on the shore
of blue Lake Kieve in the evening
and listen, grieving
as something stirs and turns within you.

Not knowing why you linger in the dark.
Not able even to guess
from what you are excluded.

THE WETNESS

I wanted to write a simple poem
about the wetness between a woman's legs

and what kind of holy moment it is
when the man's hand quietly moves south

over the smooth curve of the belly
into the shade of that other hemisphere

and his fingertips find hidden in dark fur
the seam already expectant in its moistness.

I wanted to write about that moment
as if it was full of incense,

and monks holding up their Latin like a torch
deep inside a cavern of Gregorian chant

But if I write that, someone will inevitably say what
has that romantic foofaw got to do

with the beleaguered realities of love
or with the biological exigencies of lubrication

or with the vast, retarded hierarchies of human suffering?

And someone else will add
that the man's hand
represents the historical hunter-gatherer tradition

invading the valley of the woman's body
with the obsolete presumptions of possession

whereas the woman's body is known to be
the starting place of agriculture,

doing just fine thank you by itself

until the man's hand barges into her Shangri-La,
and tramples her zucchinis and tomatoes.

But to the man, the wetness is a blessing
for which there is no history;

a coin that cannot be counterfeit,

And when the man's fingers reach it
the wetness ripples upward like a volt,
a cool wind, an annunciation

and he tastes it,
as if his hand was a tongue
he had sent ahead of him.

I wanted to write a poem about
                    the wetness
between a woman's legs

but it got complicated in language.
It is a wetness the man would make for himself
                                        if he could

—if he could only reach
                    that part of himself
which has been dry for years;

if he could only show
        a part of what he feels
                when he finds out

he is not a thousand miles from home.
That he will not have to go

into the country of desire alone.

AN ORDINARY NIGHT IN ATHENS, OHIO

Those children in pajamas
in the big suburban houses

are not dreaming
of fireflies in jars,

nor model cars,
but of fist-fighting

on Mars
in bodies not their own.

They are not feeding the hamster
small bits of lettuce

and changing its name
from Joe to Josephine, and back,

but sprinting over the rooftops
of burning Dairy Queens

and aiming shoulder-launched rockets
into shopping malls.

They are not dreaming
of taking the quiz

and getting fatally hung up
on the answer to question four,

but of nine school buses
wrapped in yellow flame,

and of playmates they knew
in second grade

floating face down
over the dimes and tarnished pennies

in the wishing fountain.

WINE DARK SEA

"'Wine dark sea'—that's from Homer, you know,"
my father said, about a book that I was reading
called *The Wine Dark Sea*.

I was furious at the old idiot
for presuming that he might know something about literature
that wasn't already mine.

So I've grown up to be one of those people
who gets angry at trees
for behaving like trees,

who kneels in hotel rooms and bangs his head
softly against the carpet, asking for help,
another kind of room service.

I remember the time he told me he had read
Don Quixote in the original French.
When I wrecked the car, it was him I called collect.

At Christmas I'll send him a case of grapefruit.
When he dies, I'll fly to the funeral
with a whole unpublished text inside of me

which I'll reread en route,
making certain overdue corrections.
Looking out the window at the Old World

passing below,
as dark and unknown as the sea.

THE COMPLEX SENTENCE

The kind Italian driver of the bus to Rome
invited her to his house—she was obviously
hungry— and gave her sandwiches
and raped her.

All those years ago: she smiles
while telling it—contemptuous,
somehow
of her stupid younger self,

who still drags behind her like a can.
Grammar is great
but who will write the sentence
that includes the story of her wound

and how she thought her bad Italian
was at fault, and
how it took a year for her to say
the word for what had happened
                                        in her head?

But that's why
we invented the complex sentence,
so we could stand at a distance,

making slight adjustments
in the view,
while trying hard to track
the twisty, ever-turning plot:

the loneliness of what we did;
the loneliness
        of what was done to us.

WRONG QUESTION

Are you alright? she asks, wrinkling her brow,
and I think how unfair that question is,

how it rises up and hangs there in the air
like a Welcome sign shining in the dark:

Are you alright? is all she has to say
with that faint line between her eyebrows
                                that signifies concern,

and her soft, moral-looking mouth,
and I feel as if I have fallen off my bike

and she wants to take care of my skinned knee
back at her apartment.

Are you alright? she says,

and all the belts begin to move inside my factory
and all the little citizens of me

set aside their tasks, stand up and start to hymn
their fifteen-hour version of the *Messiah of Unhappy Me.*

All-Right?

I thought I was alright before she asked,

but now I find that I have never been alright.
There is something soft and childish at my core

I have not been able to eradicate.
And yet— that is the question I keep answering.

A HISTORY OF HIGH HEELS

It's like God leaned down long ago and said,
to a woman who was just standing around,
"How would you like a pair of shoes
that shoves the backs of your feet up about four inches
so you balance always on your tiptoes

and your spine roller-coasters forward, then back,
so that even when you are spin-doctoring a corporate merger
or returning from your father's funeral in Florida,
your rump sticks out in a fertility announcement

and your chest is pushed out a little bit in front of you,
the way that majorettes precede a marching band?"

No, I shouldn't have said that—I'm sorry.
It's just my curdled bitterness talking; it's just my disappointment flaring up
                              in a little brush fire of misogyny,
in a toxic blaze of misdirected scorn—

because today is one of those days when I am starting to suspect
that sex was just a wild-goose chase
in which I honk-honk-honked away
        three-quarters of my sweet, unconscious life.

Now my hair is gray, and I'm in the Philadelphia airport,
where women are still walking past me endlessly

with that *clickety-clack, clickety-clack,*
flipping their hair and licking their teeth,

while underneath my own shoes
I suddenly can feel the emptiness of space;
and over my head, light falling from the sky
that all these years
I might have been leaning back

to gaze at and long for and praise.

SUMMIT MEETING

The Germans fly in the day before
and get the hotel rooms promised to the Palestinians.
The Bolivians are nervous but expectant,
having promised not to make a scene this time.

They say that money isn't passionate but
you can see the way it pulses
in the groin of the rich country
right before it expels a big aid package

into the groin of the needy secondary country
and how the face of the senator flushes and grows hot
as he bends to sign the paper
for the symbolic transfer of the funds.

Have you ever heard the sound a peso makes
when it scurries inside a Euro and holds still?
or the chamber music of distant dollars turning
into zlotys into deutschmarks into yen?

It is a symphony now being played
by an orchestra of diplomats on corporate cello,
whose strings are numbered bank accounts
plucked by supercomputer fingers.

At night, if you put your ear against the sidewalk
you can hear the clean rustle of the cash
rushing through the pipes,
pouring from one vault to the next,

into bigger and bigger pockets.
It was all designed so long ago, no one
remembers why—to keep misery organized?
In the mansions on the hill

the rich are taking showers:
turning the handles of silver faucets
to get a clean cold gush of cash.
Over and over they appear upon the balcony
to wave, or make a speech;

and there are roses in their cheeks:
roses manufactured from crushed hopes
which changing hands has turned
into the fragrance of fresh flowers.

DECEMBER, WITH ANTLERS

Why are people wearing antlers in the hospital cafeteria?
—Because it's Christmas, silly.

Can't you hear the sleigh bells
drifting down like pesticide from all the hidden speakers?

Mr. Johansson says he doesn't get paid
                                enough to wear a Santa hat,
but everybody else just goes along with it.

It's winter, the elevators ding, the stunned relatives get off and on.
If it is Indiana or Ohio, they bring food.

No one sees the drama of the not-dead flowers,
taken from the room of the deceased
and thrown onto the trash.

Was it Stevens, or Corinthians?: "We make our dwelling
on the slope of a volcano."

You have to admire the ones who stand outside to smoke,
studying the parking lot,
all James-Dean casual with their IV poles.

If you could see them through my eyes, they all have antlers.
Human beings are tough—

with their obesity, their chemo and their scars,
their courage in the face of dark prognosis.

Tough as Rudolf-fucking carcinoma.

Look. Here come the three wise women,
up the escalator, bearing Jell-O.

WRITE WHITER

Obviously, it's a category I've been made aware of
                                        from time to time.

It's been pointed out that my characters eat a lot of lightly-braised asparagus
and get FedEx packages almost daily.

Yet I dislike being thought of as a writer of whiteness.
I never wanted to be pigeonholed like that.

When I find my books in the "White Literature" section of the bookstore,
                                dismay is what I feel—

I thought I was talking about other, larger things.

Tax refunds, Spanish lessons, premature ejaculation;
meatloaf and sitcoms; the fear of perishing.

I know some readers need to see their lives reflected from the page—
It lets them know they aren't alone.

The art it takes to make that kind of comfort
                                is not something I look upon with scorn.

But after awhile, you start to feel like white
                                is all you'll ever be.

And gradually, after all the struggling against,
after tasting your own fear of being

only what you are,
you accept—

Then, with fresh determination, you lean forward again.
You write whiter and whiter.

THERE IS NO WORD

There isn't a word for walking out of the grocery store
with a gallon jug of milk in a plastic sack
that should have been bagged in double layers

—so that before you are even out the door
you feel the weight of the jug dragging
the bag down, stretching the thin

plastic handles longer and longer
and you know it's only a matter of time until
the strap breaks or the bottom suddenly splits
and spills its contents to the ground.

There is no single, particular, unimpeachably precise word
for that vague sensation of something
moving away from you
as it exceeds its elastic capacity

which is too bad because that is the word
I would like to use to describe
standing on the street and chatting with a friend,

as the awareness gradually dawns in me that he
is no longer a friend,
but only an acquaintance,

until this moment as we say goodbye,
when I think we share a feeling of relief,
an unspoken recognition

that we have reached the end of a pretense,
—though to tell the truth,
what I already am thinking

is that Language deserves the credit—
 how it will stretch just so much and no farther;
how there are some holes it will not cover up;

how it will move, if not inside, then
around the circumference
of almost anything—

how, over the years, it has given me
back all the hours and days, all the
plodding love and faith, all the

misunderstandings and secrets and mistakes
I have willingly poured into it.

APPLICATION FOR RELEASE
FROM THE DREAM

This is my favorite kind of weather, this cloudy autumn-ness—
When long wool coats make shoplifting easy,

and you can see, in all the windows of the stores,
the nipples of the mannequins pushing through their warm cashmere.

I keep the wise books on my shelves, and take them down to read
but I no longer believe in their power to transform.

What is it? Maybe all the mystery anyone could need
is already right here, inside my abdomen

like the fine tremble of the filament inside a bulb.

When I came to this place initially,
I thought I would never be able to bear

the false laughter and the lies, hearing
the same stories told again and again

by the same people in the same words.
But that is just an example of the kind of bad thoughts that visit me.

Ten years after being cheated by Jim, of *Jim's Bookstore*,
I still am angry, though I said nothing at the time.

Sometimes maybe it is better to be mute—to take long walks,
to pull dead weeds from between the paving stones.

Outside, a faint mist falling from the low, steel-colored sky.
and the red light inside the strangely glowing trees.

"Thank you for the honesty of being afraid," I say to myself out loud,
                    "afraid of things you do not understand."

Exhausted then, I fell asleep. But I awoke knowing the rules:

If you aren't learning, you haven't been paying attention.
If you have nothing to say, it is because your heart is closed.

PROPORTION

The attorney collects a fee of seven million
for getting eighteen million back

from the widow of the CEO
whose corporation stole three billion

from ten thousand
stockholders and employees.

She has to go down to one Mercedes
and take driving lessons.

The radio said expect delays,
but five thousand years for justice
                            just seems ridiculous.

What I heard from behind me at the baseball game
"We can't see crap from over here"—it seemed
                            so true of us.

The two young actresses flip a coin
to see who will get to play the cancer patient

because they know
the worst fate makes the best role

and that dying can be good for your career.

One of them will go to Hollywood and be a star.
The other will move to Cincinnati,

and take photos of her twins
running back and forth through the sprinkler

in shorts,

soaking wet, shrieking with delight.

ODE TO THE REPUBLIC

It's going to be so great when America is just a second fiddle
and we stand on the sidelines and watch the big boys slug it out.

Old men reading the *Times* on benches in Central Park
                will smile and say, "Let France take care of it."

Farmers in South Carolina will have bumper stickers that read
"One nation, with vegetables for all"; and "USA:
                Numero Uno for grade triple-A tomatoes!"

America, you big scary baby, don't you know that
          when you pounded your chest like that in public
                    it just embarrassed us?
When you lied to yourself on television,
                we looked down at our feet;

When your left hand turned into a claw,
          when you hammered the little country down
              and sang the pledge of allegiance,
I put on my new sunglasses
        and stared at the church across the street.

I thought I had to go down with you,
              hating myself in red white and blue,

learning to say "I'm sorry," in more and more foreign languages.

But now the end of our dynasty has arrived
             and I feel calm and curiously free.

It's so good to be unimportant
It's nice to sit on the shore of the Potomac
                    and watch time take back half of everything.

It's a relief to take the dog for a walk
            without frightening the neighbors.

My country, 'tis of thee I sing:
            There are worse things than being
                                second burrito,

minor player, ex-bigshot, former VIP, drinking decaf
            in the nursing home for downsized superpowers.

Like a Navajo wearing a cowboy hat, may you learn
                                to love the ironies.

May you look into the mirror and see your doubleness:
                        old blue eyes in a brown face.

May your women finally lay down
                    the law: No more war on a school night.

May your shame at failure be cushioned by the oldest kind of chemotherapy:
                        stage after stage of acceptance.

May someone learn to love you again.

May you sit on the porch with the other countries
                in the late afternoon,
                        and talk about chickens and rain.

SUMMER DUSK

I put in my goddamn hearing aid
in order to listen to a bird that sounds
like the side of a drinking glass
struck lightly by a fork

and try not to hate a life that
that dips you in Time like a teabag
over and over and pulls you up
each year a slightly different color.

Yet I like this hour when the air goes soft
and leaves stir with relief at the end
of their labor of being leaves.
"What a piece of work is man," I say,

not knowing Hamlet said it first—
"how noble in reason, how infinite in faculties,
in form and moving how express; in apprehension how like an angel,
and yet, to me, the quintessence of dust!"

This hour of the evening
with a little infinity inside,
like an amnesty from the interminable
condition of being oneself.

This half-hour when you look out
and see that it is sweet.
Even in my deafness I can hear
the bird whose name I do not know

speaking to someone in the dusk.

AUBADE

The moon is going down, innocent and pale as a wafer
dissolving in the mouth of a Catholic

and those first, high-flying birds of dawn
are only faintly visible, like a photograph developing.

Just off stage, the rooster someone keeps illegally
in the city crows its magnificent cry,

blessing, who knows, maybe the child
just conceived inside a woman's body.

Such tranquility—the neighbors haven't started fighting
yet, nor their loud hyena laughter.

It's peaceful as a golf course in Jerusalem,
remembering when it used to be a meadow.

And we still love each other, in a way that makes us
tolerant, alert, perhaps a little vain

but also, we are getting older.
Come over here, darling,

and put your hand on my head
and tell me if you think this is a tumor.

69071603R00031

Made in the USA
Lexington, KY
24 October 2017